Peyote Stitch for Beginner and Beyo

Sheila Root, PhD
Master Jeweler

©2014 Root's Beads
Root's Beads
9235 S Village Shop Drive
Sandy Utah 84094
801-790-2323

Text, designs, and photography ©2014 Sheila Root

All rights reserved. No portion of this work may be reproduced or used in any form or by any means –graphical, electronic, digital or mechanical including photocopying, photographing, recording, taping of information on storage and retrieval systems– without the written consent of Root's Beads.

The written instructions, photographs, designs and projects in this book are intended for the personal use of the reader, which would include making pieces to sell at local fairs or as gifts but not mass produced for sale through other venues such as internet sites or catalogs.

Sheila Root is a beading artist and co-owner of Root's Beads. She has been in the bead business for over twenty years and has taught hundreds of students in seed bead techniques and basic and advanced stringing techniques as well as wire techniques. A former university professor with degrees in design and a certificate in Master Jewelry, she has been designing and selling "wearable art" for many years. Sheila also has a background in textile arts and was a founding member of FiberRoots, participated in many gallery exhibitions both in group shows and as featured artist. She has written several other books including *Graphics for Interior Space, Beaded Ornament Covers: A Beginner's Guide, Beaded Ornament Covers Book Two, Beaded Ornament Covers Book Three, Wire Wrapping Stones* (1st edition), *Wire Wrapping Stones and Beads* (2nd Edition), *Handmade, not Homemade: A Bead Stringing Guide,* and *Spirit of the West: Amulet Bags in Peyote Stitch.* This book is one of a series of patterns for Peyote stitch. Watch for other titles coming soon.

Contents

Basic Tips on Peyote Stitch...page 1
Flat Even Count..page 5
Flat Odd Count...page 7
Two-drop Peyote Stitch..page 9
Increase and Decrease on the Ends of Rows..................page 10
Increase and Decrease in the Middle of Rows................page 13
Flat Diagonal Peyote Stitch..page 14
Tubes from Flat Peyote...page 16
Spiral Tubes...page 18
Dimensional Peyote...page 19
    Shaped Flat Peyote
    Shaped Spiral Tubes
    Ruffles
    Beaded Beads
Peyote Bezels...page 24
Projects

Even Count Peyote Bracelet
Page 28

Odd count Peyote Pendant
Page 29

Peyote Bead Bracelet
Page 31

Cabochon Pendant with Beaded Bezel
Page 33

Ruffled Peyote Bracelet
Page 36

Simple Spiral Bracelet
Page 39

Necklace with Dimensional Spiral Accents
Page 40

Diagonal Peyote Bracelet
Page 42

Russian Leaf Embellishment
Page 44

Zigzag Cuff Bracelet
Page 48

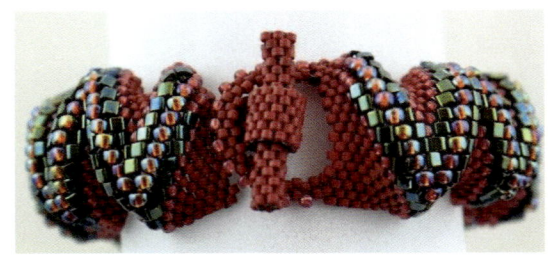

Basic Tips on Peyote Stitch

Peyote stitch is a very useful bead weaving stitch which is probably why it has been used throughout the world for many years. There is evidence that it may even have been used by the ancient Egyptians. The modern name of peyote stitch derives from its use by Native American people in their ritual ceremonies. It is also sometimes called gourd stitch because of its use in decorating gourds. But whatever you choose to call it, this stitch can be used with odd or even numbers of beads, flat, circular, diagonal, ruffled, or freeform. Start with the basics, work your way through the stitches and patterns and by the time you finish this book you will be an expert on the stitch! So have fun and let's get started.

Thread Choice

Always use a good quality beading thread for peyote stitch. Some projects can be very hard on your thread. There are many manufacturers of beading thread but there are basically two types of thread that work well for peyote stitch: flat or twisted nylon filament beading threads, and braided beading threads. The one you choose will depend on your project.

One of the braided beading threads will hold up better than nylon filament threads for large projects, especially if you like to use a long thread to avoid knots. The braided threads have better abrasion resistance and are less likely to fray or tangle when doing a large project.

Braided threads usually come in neutral colors including white or clear for light colors and grey or khaki green for darker colors. The only place the thread color really shows is on the edges of a design. Therefore choose your thread color to blend with the color that is most prominent on the edges. About a 6 pound test or 8 pound test braided thread works well and will fit through a size 10 beading needle.

The non-braided beading threads are fine for some smaller peyote projects and come in a much wider selection of colors to coordinate with your beads. These threads are usually softer and have a nicer drape but the braided threads are easier to keep a tight tension if you are doing a dimensional piece that needs to hold its shape.

Everyone has their own brand preference for thread but you should experiment and see which ones work best for you. Remember that no one thread may be perfect for all projects.

Never use sewing thread. It is not designed for bead work and will not hold up well.

Knots

Some instructions will tell you that simply working the thread back into the beading will be enough to secure it. Don't always believe it! After years of seeing my customers broken hearted because the project they made with this method fell apart, I highly recommend knotting your threads.

You can leave the beginning thread hanging until you have worked a ways past it or even until you reach the end of the project. Work it back into the beads, but make several half hitch knots as you do to secure the thread firmly in place. Then work the thread through a few more beads before you trim off the excess. Pull the thread snug after each knot and the knots will disappear between the beads. Repeat with the ending thread.

If you need to add more thread in the middle of a project, leave the first thread hanging and start the new one. Tie the ends of the two threads firmly together. After you have worked a ways past the splice, put the needle back on the thread and work each piece of thread back into the beadwork, pulling the knot into the beads. Trim off the excess thread. Never trim the thread right up against the knot because that may cause it to slip open.

Gluing knots is optional but usually not necessary and will increase the size of the knot making it harder to hide in the beads. Some people singe off the thread ends but I have also seen this destroy a project if not done properly. Practice on some samples before singing threads on a finished project.

Beads

Just about any kind of seed beads can be used for peyote stitch: rocailles (round), cubes, cylinder beads, triangles, hex cuts, etc. For beginners, it is usually easier to start with beads with flat ends such as Japanese cylinder beads, cubes, or hex cuts. These beads fit together like little tiles. Rocailles of any size can be used, however they tend to be shaped more like a little donut so they don't fall into place quite as easily.

The sample on the left used hex cut beads; the ends fit tightly together.

The sample on the right used rocailles; the rounded edges leave more space between the beads.

Note that the beads in both illustrations are size 8/0 but the shape of the sample is different even though each piece used the same number of beads. If you are working a pattern that has specified a particular shape of beads, the finished project may differ considerably if you substitute a different shape of bead without compensating for the length/width ratio difference.

Many peyote projects will need a variety of bead sizes or shapes while others can be made entirely with one type of bead. Changing sizes can help to create dimension or alter shapes. Changing bead shapes can add interest and dimension, and also alter shapes.

Tension is very important when working in peyote stitch, especially shaped pieces like diagonal stitching or three dimensional pieces. It will help keep your tension snug if you hold your work between your thumb and forefinger. Wrap the working thread back over your forefinger and hold it against your forefinger with your other fingers. Release your grip on your thread just as you tighten up the next stitch.

Stopper Beads

A stopper bead serves as a knot at the beginning of your beadwork to keep your beads from sliding off the end of the thread. Unlike a knot, it is easily removed when you don't need it any more. Use a small bead, usually an 11/0, string it onto your thread down to the point where you want to begin your beadwork, leaving the desired length of thread beyond the stopper bead.

Run the needle back up through this bead two or three times so that it doesn't slide. Be very careful NOT to split the thread with your needle. Press the bead up with your finger so that you will run the needle through the empty space in the bead rather than through the thread.

When the bead is no longer needed, loosen the threads with your needle and pull the stopper off.

Following Patterns

As a beginning student of peyote stitch, it is best to work a sample of each style without any pattern. Once you have mastered the technique then you can move on to patterns.

Diagonal or vertical stripes are the simplest patterns to begin with. Move up to geometrics. When you have mastered following these simple patterns then you can move up to more complex designs of flowers, animals, etc.

If working from a diagram, lay a ruler or stiff paper across the pattern at the bottom edge of the row you are working on. As you complete each row put a little check mark beside it so you don't lose your place if your ruler gets bumped. After each row, move the ruler up one row, remembering that one row is only half a bead high.

Patterns can also be easier to follow if you lay the beads out one row at a time. Place the ruler across the pattern row. Pick out the beads in the row and lay them out in order on your beading mat. Work the row of peyote stitch, then check off that row. Move the ruler up to the next row and repeat.

Flat Even Count Peyote Stitch

Peyote stitch has many variations but the easiest place to start is with flat even count peyote. Once you have mastered flat even count then you can get creative with other variations of the stitch.

Working in Peyote stitch is kind of like laying bricks sideways; the beads are staggered and laid in place one at a time. To begin, all the beads from Row 1 and Row 2 are strung on first, alternating the beads from the first and second row of the design. From that point on the beads are added one bead at a time. If the pattern is 60 beads wide you will begin by stringing on 60 beads; each subsequent row will then add just 30 beads.

Row 1 (green) & row 2 (blue):

String on all beads for row 1 and 2, starting with the first bead from row 2.

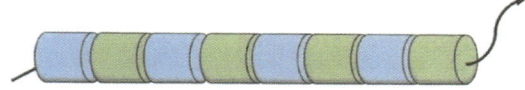

Row 3 (tan):

String on the first bead from row 3.

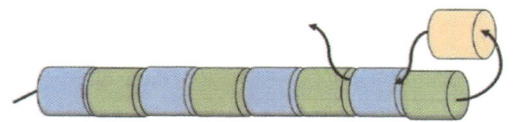

Run the needle back through the last bead from row 2, skipping over the bead from row 1.

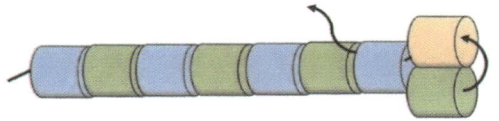

When you pull the bead snug it will sit side by side with the first bead from row 1.

First two rows worked in Japanese cylinder beads and the beginning of row 3:

Continue adding the rest of the beads from row 3, each time skipping over the beads from row 1 and running the needle through the next bead from row 2.

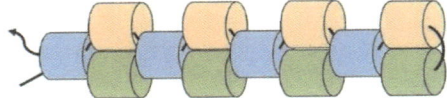

When you pull the thread snug it should look like a little hop scotch game.

Row 4 (yellow):

String on the first bead from row 4.

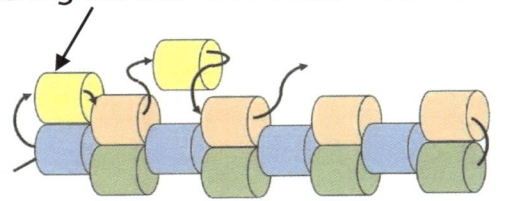

Run the needle back through the last bead from row 3.

Continue adding the beads from row 4, each time running the needle through the next bead from row 3.

Once you have completed row 3, the rest of the rows are easy because each bead from the previous row sticks up, making it easy to run the needle through the next bead.

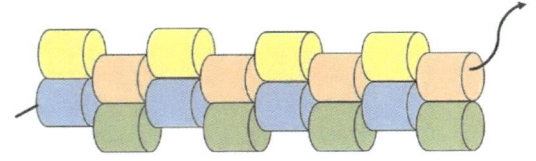

Continue adding rows until the piece reaches the desired length. If a pattern calls for a certain number of rows, remember that each row is ½ step up. The sample on the right has six rows.

Flat Odd Count Peyote

Even count peyote stitch means there are an even number of beads in each row, making it easy to turn the corner and start the next row.

Odd count peyote stitch has an odd number of beads in each row. An odd count requires extra work at the end of each odd numbered row, making it a little trickier for beginners.

Most projects can be worked in even count peyote, but odd count needs to be used if you have a pattern such as this one with a definite center line. This design would be lopsided in even count.

To begin a flat odd count peyote pattern string on all the beads from row one (green) and row two (blue), this time starting with the first bead from row one.

The third row is worked the same as the third row in even count peyote stitch until you get to the last bead.

At the end of the third row it is necessary to take an extra stitch to anchor the last bead of row three and begin row four.

String on the next to last bead for row 3 (10) and run the needle back through the last bead from row 2 (2) and the end bead from row 1 (1) (right to left as shown).

With the thread coming out of the end bead from row 1 (1), pick up the first bead for row 3 (11).

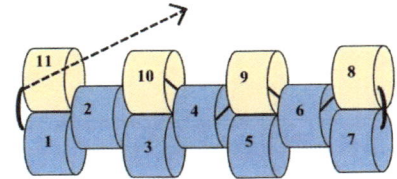

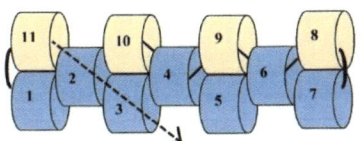

Run the needle down through the last bead of row 2 (2) and the second bead of row 1 (3).

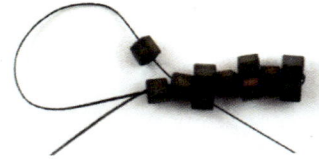

With the thread coming out of (3), run the needle right to left through (10), (2), and (1).

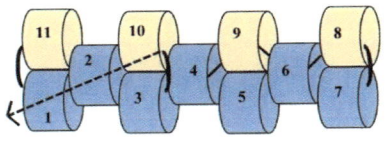

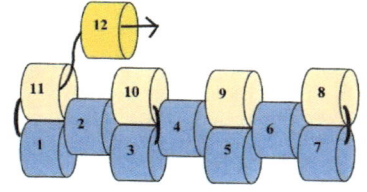

Run the needle left to right through (11).

You are now ready to begin the 4th row (12).

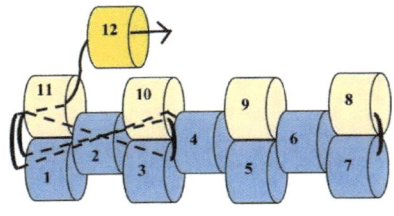

If you put all the steps together in one diagram you can see that you are making a figure 8.

Remember that only one end of odd count peyote stich requires the extra stitch. The odd numbered rows are started the same as in even count peyote. The even numbered rows require the figure 8 stitch.

Continue adding rows. Each odd numbered row begins the same as an even count row and ends with the extra figure 8 stitch to anchor the end bead.

Two-Drop Peyote Stitch

Peyote Stitch can be worked in increments of more than one bead at a time. Two-drop peyote stitch is worked the same as peyote worked one bead at a time, however each stitch uses two beads instead of one. Working two beads at a time speeds the process up and gives a little different look.

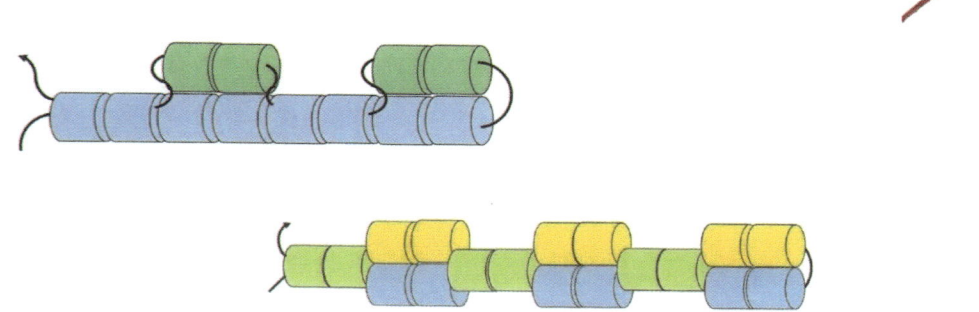

Odd count peyote stitch is worked the same as single bead odd count peyote stitch. Just use two beads instead of one.

To make the ends a bit more sturdy try using a single bead at the end of the rows and two-drop in between.

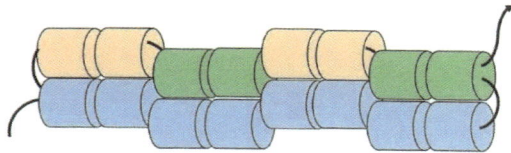

Two drop peyote can also be combined with single bead peyote for a different look. Just alternate a stitch with one bead with a stitch with two beads. This creates a different texture.

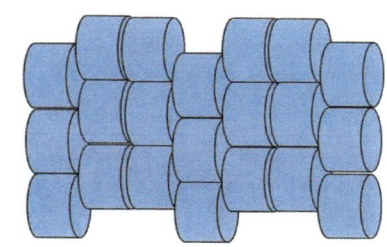

Increase and Decrease at End of Rows

To decrease at the end of the row:

Exit the needle one bead before the end of the row and continue with the next row.

This decreases the width of the beadwork by two columns. To decrease the width by four columns, exit two beads before the end of the row. Using this method the width of the beadwork can be decreased by any number of columns in multiples of two.

To decrease the width by just one bead:

At the end of an even count row, instead of adding the next bead, run the needle back through the last bead of the row before.

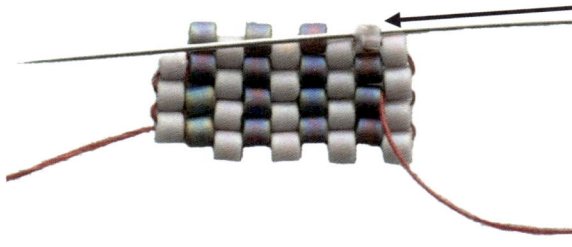

Take another stitch through the last bead added from the top row.

Pull the thread snug so that it drops down between the beads.

The thread is now in position to complete another row.

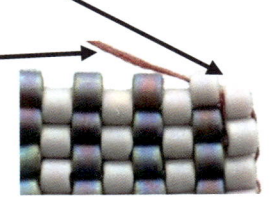

The thread illustrated is a contrasting color to show up in the photos, but if you use a matching color it will nearly disappear.

This single column decrease leaves a smoother edge than a two-column decrease.

Single bead decrease on odd count:

Bring the thread out one bead short of the end.

Run the needle back through the next bead below where the thread is coming out.

Run the needle back through the next bead in the top row.

You are now ready to bead the next row.

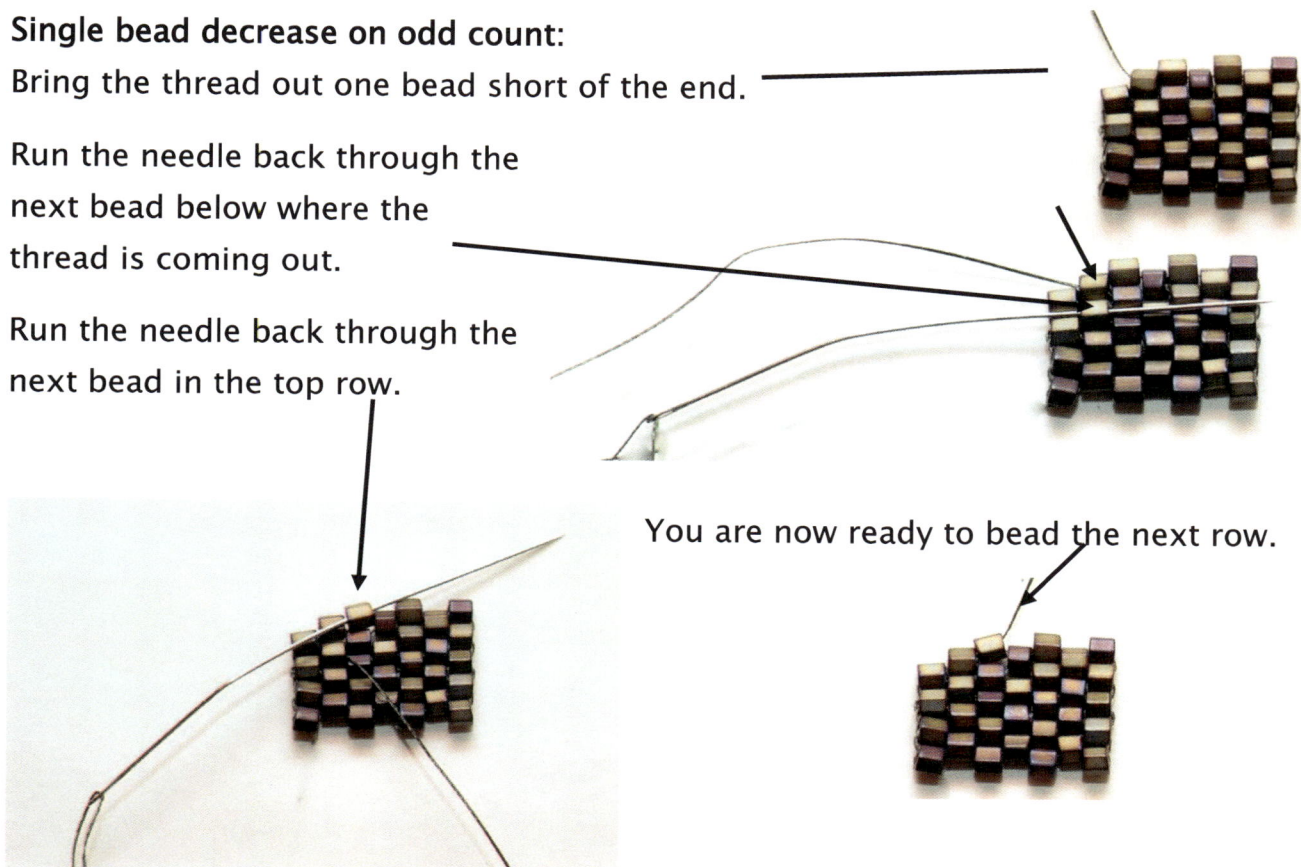

Increase at the end of a row:

String on three more beads beyond the end of the existing row. Run the needle back through the first of these three beads. Continue the row as usual.
This adds two columns to the width of your beadwork.

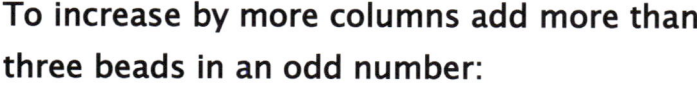

To increase by more columns add more than three beads in an odd number:

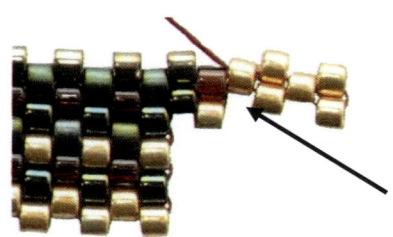

To add four columns, string on five beads, run the needle back through the third of these new beads, add a sixth bead and run the needle back through the first of the new beads. Continue the row as usual.

Using this method any number of columns can be added in groups of two.

This example shows an increase of two columns followed by an increase of four more columns.

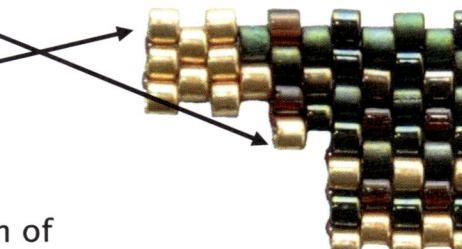

Increase by one bead column:

To add just one column of beads, exit the end of the row and string on two beads.

Run the needle back through the end bead from the previous row, right to left, as shown.

Catch the needle under the thread between the beads.

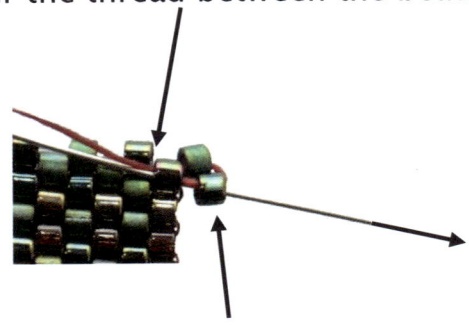

Run the needle back left to right through the same bead and the bottom one of the two new beads.

Run the needle back right to left through the top one of the two new beads.

Proceed with the rest of the row in the usual manner.

Increasing and Decreasing in Middle of Rows

Increasing and decreasing in the middle of a row can change the shape of a piece of beadwork. It can be accomplished by adding and subtracting beads or by changing the size of the bead at the point of increase or decrease.

To increase:

At the point of increase, use two beads instead of one.

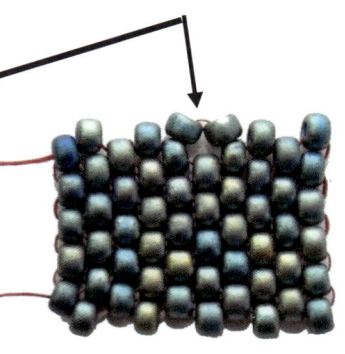

Work the next row normally except add a bead between the two beads in the double stitch from the previous row.

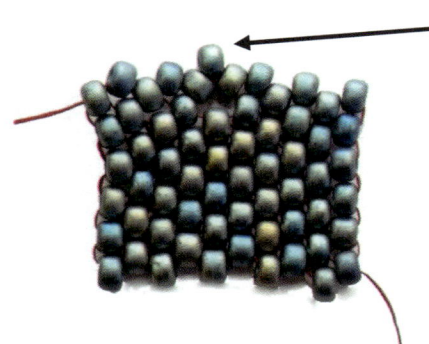

Work the next row normally. Notice that now you have two more beads in the row than you had previously.

To decrease:

At the point of decrease run the needle between two beads from the existing row without adding the usual bead between them.

On the next row treat the condensed space as if it were a normal stitch.

Notice that there are now two fewer beads than there were when you started.

Flat Diagonal Peyote

Diagonal peyote is a versatile stitch for making straps and bracelets. It is easy to alter the pattern of the diagonal and to embellish the edges for a different look. Diagonal peyote is also the foundation for making Russian leaves, shown here in the example at the left.

Start by working three rows of flat even count peyote. (Illustration is ten beads wide but this can be any width you prefer.)

Work the fourth row in the regular manner but exit one bead before the end of the row. This will create the first decrease to start the diagonal.

Work the fifth row, exiting the last bead from the fourth row. String on 3 more beads and run the needle back through the first of these three to make the increase and start the sixth row.

14

Work row six, exiting one bead before the end of the previous row for the next decrease.

Continue adding rows.

Decrease one bead on the right end of each row and increase on the left end by adding the sequence of three beads.

Add rows until you have reached your desired length.

Diagonal stitch can also be worked in groups, creating more of a stepped effect.

Work four rows (or any desired number of rows) in peyote stitch then make one decrease on the right and one increase on the left.

Work another block of four rows and repeat the decrease and increase.

Continue until the strip reaches the desired length.

Tubes from Flat Peyote

Tubes are easy to make from flat peyote stitch. They work well for short sections of tube, such as beaded beads. This method tends to produce a rather stiff piece of work so it doesn't work as well for a long section of tube. If you want a tubular rope for a necklace, see the next section.

String on an even number of beads. The length of this string of beads will determine the length of the beaded tube.

Work an even number of rows in flat even count peyote stitch. The number of rows will determine the diameter of the tube. Beginning and ending threads will be on opposite corners.

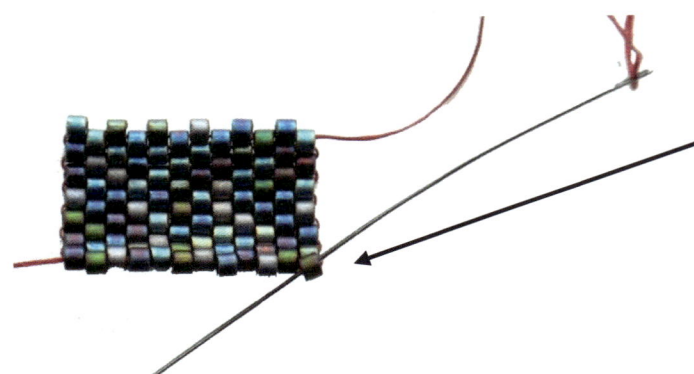

To "zip" up the side seam, run the needle through the end bead on the opposite side. Pull the thread up to begin the tube.

Now run the needle through the next bead on the opposite side.

16

Continue stitching through the raised beads back and forth between the two sides.

As you snug up the thread the seam will pull together and the joint will disappear.

Tie the two thread ends together.

Work the ends back into the beadwork and trim off excess thread.

When you string the beads onto flex wire or a headpin, slide seed beads down inside the tube so that it stays centered on your beading wire and doesn't get flattened. Use enough beads to fill the space without protruding beyond the ends of the tube. The size of seed beads needed will depend on the diameter of your tube.

The sample shown here was worked in size 11/0 Japanese cylinder beads with 14 rows. This makes a tube about 5mm diameter, and uses 10/0 cylinder beads to fill the inside space.

Spiral Tubes

Spiral tubes are also easy to make and are much more flexible than flat peyote tubes, making them better suited for longer ropes of beadwork.

Start by stringing on an odd number of beads. The length of this string will determine the diameter of the spiral tube.

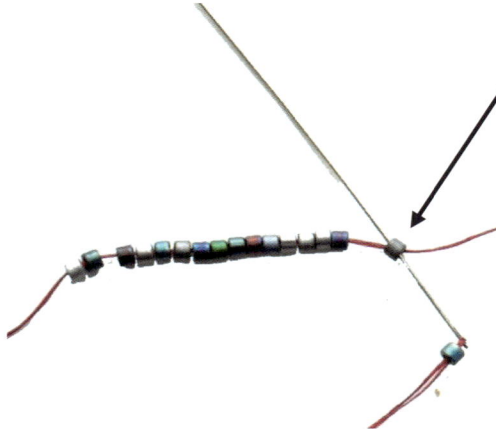

Run the needle back through the first bead.

When you pull the thread snug this will form it into a circle.

Add another bead, skip over one bead and run the needle through the next bead.

Continue around the circle. This will form the first three rows of peyote stitch.

String on another bead and begin the next round of beads.

As you pull the thread snug it will form a circular tube shape.

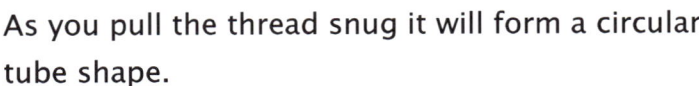

There will be a slight spiral to the tube because each row is slanted up from the last.

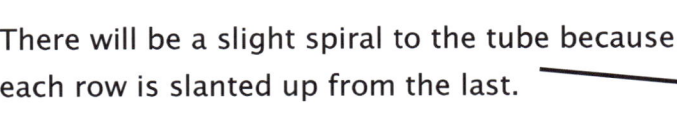

Some people find it easier to work with a form inside the spiral. This can be a pencil, a drinking straw or any other object that fits the size of your tube.

Dimensional Peyote

Note: Dimensional peyote stitches rely on a snug tension for the beadwork to take the proper shape. If your tension is too loose the beads will just lie flat with space between them. So keep a firm grip on your beadwork and cinch up that thread!

Shaped Flat Peyote Stitch:

To create a raised portion in an otherwise flat piece of peyote stitch, use increasing and decreasing bead sizes. The example demonstrated will create a raised diagonal stripe in the beadwork using three sizes of beads.

Start with a few rows of flat even count peyote in the smallest (1st) size bead (shown in 11/0 cylinder beads).

Begin the next row with one bead a size larger (2nd size, 11/0 rocaille shown) and then complete the rest of the row with the 1st size bead.

Work back across the row normally but add another of the 2nd size bead diagonally next to the first one.

Start the next row with the 3rd size bead (8/0 rocaille shown) and then take the next stitch with the 2nd size bead. Complete the row with the 1st size bead.

Work the next row with the 1st size, then use the 2nd and 3rd size beads diagonally next to the same sizes in the previous row.

11/0   8/0   11/0

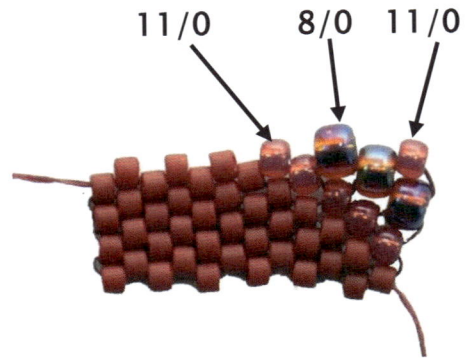

Continue adding rows, each time using the size bead that matches diagonally to the row below. Decrease the bead size after you cross the center of the raised portion: as shown, the raised portion has an 11/0 on each side of the 8/0 to create the raised ridge in the otherwise flat piece of peyote stitch.

Work the diagonal until you are all the way back to only the 1st size bead again.

Diagonals like this can be used singly, or in repeated rows or reversed to make a zigzag such as this sample shown.

Any number of bead sizes can be used as long as they taper up in size. This zigzag sample used four bead sizes, including triangles. This is a flatter variation of the cuff shown on page 48.

20

Shaped Spiral Tubes:

To create a raised diagonal effect in a spiral tube, select beads that taper up in size. The example shown used 3 sizes (11/0 cylinder beads, 11/0 rocailles, and 8/0 rocailles) but more sizes can be used for a more dramatic effect.

Start with a spiral ring of the 1st (smallest) size. When you are ready to start the raised spiral, substitute one bead of each ascending and descending size for the 1st size. As shown, the sample started with 13 11/0 cylinder beads, which means you will be adding 6 beads each time around. On the first shaped round there are 3 cylinder beads, one 110/ rocaille, one 8/0 rocaille, and one 11/0 rocaille.

Continue beading around the tube. Each bead that you add will be the same size as the bead that the needle is coming out of. If your needle is coming out of a cylinder, then add a cylinder; if the needle is coming out of an 11/0 rocaille, then add another 11/0 rocaille, etc.

Spirals can be very subtle with only minor size changes, or they can be more dramatic with more size variation. Note that the more subtle piece at the top uses three sizes of beads and the more dramatic piece at the bottom only uses four sizes of beads. A small change can make a big difference.

Ruffles:

Ruffles are easy to make in peyote stitch. The ruffle demonstrated here is basically just a series of increases made through bead size changes.

Choose at least three or four sizes of beads.

Start with a section of flat peyote stitch in the smallest bead size you are using (11/0 Japanese cylinder beads shown here).

 Add two rows of the 2nd size bead, pulling the new larger beads down between the smaller beads.

Add two more rows of the 3rd size.

If you have kept your tension snug the beadwork will have a nice ripple effect.

If desired, you can also enhance the edge of your ruffle by making a Pico edging of 3-5 size 15/0 rocailles to give the edge a lacey effect.

This example shows multiple ruffle edges in a necklace with crystal embellishments.

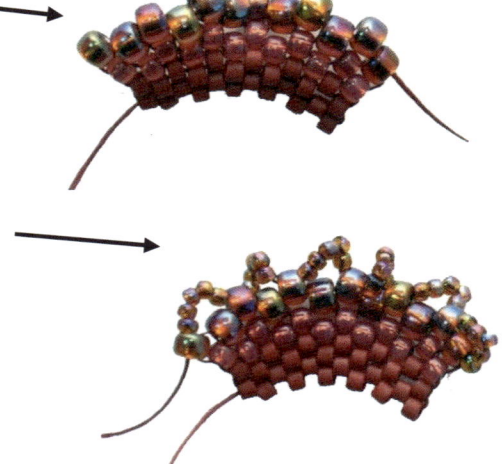

You can also make ruffles by using all one size of bead. Just make increases at random points in your rows. The more increases you make the more ripple the ruffle will have.

Beaded Beads:

Here is a simple method of making beaded beads using peyote stitch. This example is the same technique as the previous section on making beaded tube beads with peyote stitch. However, here the beads become dimensional through the use of bead size changes as you work across the row.

Start by making a section of dimensional peyote. This example used odd count peyote stitch so that the one larger bead would be in the center of the beaded bead. The smaller sizes of beads are graduated out on each side with the tiniest ones at the ends.

This example used 15/0 rocailles, 11/0 Japanese cylinder beads, 11/0 rocailles, 11/0 triangles, and 8/0 rocailles for the center row.

Zip the two sides of the bead together the same as you did making flat peyote tubes.

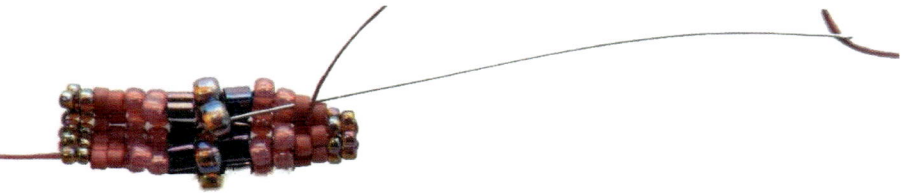

Tie off and bury the thread ends and your bead is now ready to string. Experiment with different sizes and combinations of seed beads to get different shapes of beaded beads.

Peyote Bezels

Peyote stitch can be used to create a bezel around a cabochon or donut, as shown at left.

A cabochon is a piece of stone or glass or other material that is flat on the back and rounded on the front. They can be of any shape; round, oval, square, free form, etc. Cabochons are often just referred to as cabs.

No two hand-made cabochons are exactly the same. Both the diameter and the thickness may vary. The technique shown here is the same for any size of cabochon but you may need to make modifications to fit your specific cabochon. For example, if the girdle around the edge of the cab is thicker or thinner than the one shown you may need to add extra rows of peyote on a thick edge or not do as many rows of peyote on a thinner edge.

In order to bead around the edges of a cabochon it must first be attached to a backing material. Backing material is made specifically for this purpose and is available in bead stores. There are different brands on the market and all work well. Backing is available in white or black only, but by the time you finish the cabochon the backing will be completely covered. The example shown in these instructions is worked on white backing just because it shows the thread better for the photos.

For a relatively small cabochon such as the one shown in these instructions, Japanese cylinder beads and 15/0 rocailles work best. On a much thicker piece with a raised edge like the large stone donut shown in the finished sample above, it was necessary to use size 8/0 rocailles, 11/0 rocailles, 11/0 cylinder beads, and 15/0 rocailles to capture the donut.

Glue the cabochon onto a piece of backing material. The size of the backing should be a little larger than the beaded area of your bezel. If you plan to do other beading around the finished cabochon be sure to leave enough backing for that too. Use a thick glue such as E6000. Runny glues will soak into the backing and not hold well. Smear some glue on the cabochon and press it onto the backing. Make sure the glue does not squish out the sides or you won't be able to run the needle through the glued spots. If you get too much glue scrape it off immediately before it dries.

Once the glue has dried, run a pencil around the edge of the cabochon to make a line evenly spaced just slightly away from the edge of the cab.

Tie a sewing style knot in the end of your thread. Catch the knot in the backing a little ways inside the line so that the knot doesn't get in the way when you are beading the edge. (See photo of back on pg. 27)

Bring the thread up through the backing at a point on your pencil line.

String on two Japanese cylinder beads and slide them up against the point where the thread comes out of the backing.

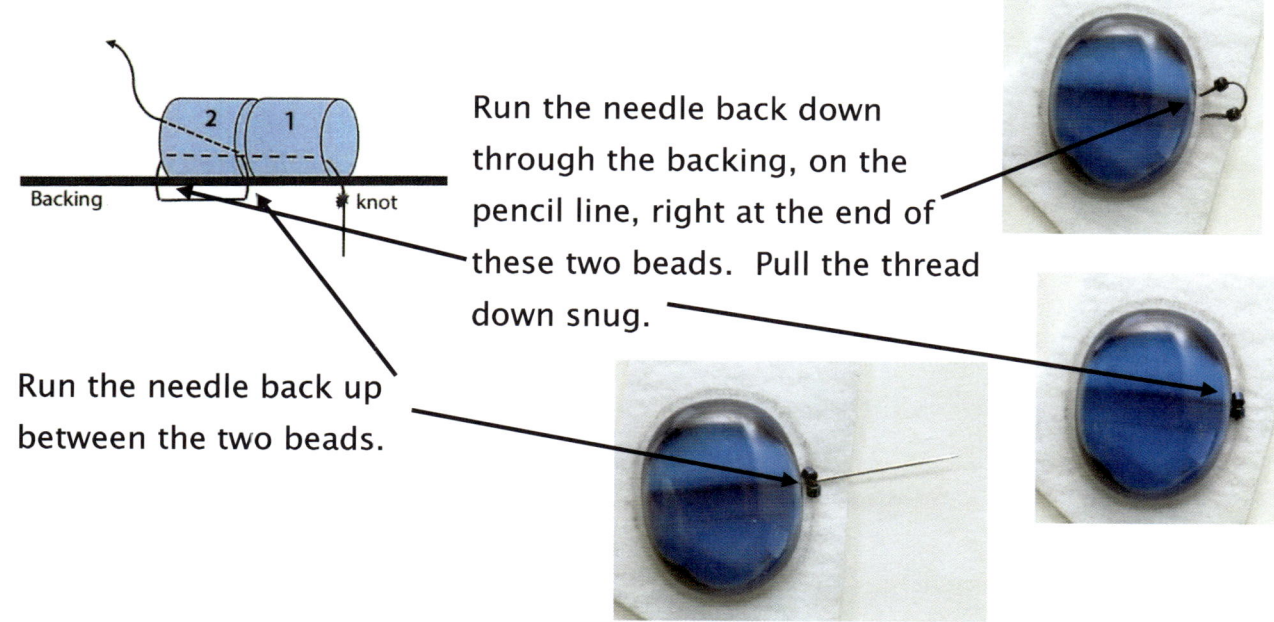

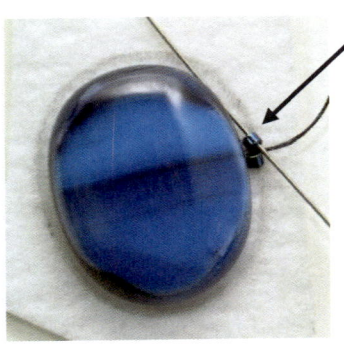

Run the needle through the second bead again.

The two beads now sit side by side with the thread ready for the next two beads.

Repeat these steps with two more beads, following the pencil line.

Continue all the way around adding two beads at a time. Space the last few beads carefully so that you end with an even number of beads.

You have now completed rows 1 and 2 for the beginning of your peyote stitch. You will notice that every second bead is firmly stitched to the backing and the first bead of each pair is somewhat loose. To create the third round of peyote stitch, begin by bringing the needle out through the first "loose" bead from row 1/row 2.

Pick up a bead on your needle, skip over the second bead (the one firmly stitched down), and run the needle through the 3rd bead (the next "loose" bead).

Continue around the row, adding one bead at a time and running the needle through the next "loose" bead, skipping over the firmly stitched beads in between the "loose" ones.

Add rows of cylinder beads until you reach the point where the cabochon starts to curve inward. In this example it took one more round of cylinder beads (4 rows total).

To curve the bezel inward over the cabochon, change to a size smaller bead for the rest of the rows, in this case 15/0 rocailles.

Two rows of 15/0 rocailles were enough to capture this glass cabochon.

The number of rows you need will depend on the size of your cabochon, the size of the beads you started with, and how much curve your cabochon has. You want enough rows to capture the cab so that it doesn't pop out of the beads but not so many that you cover up too much of the cabochon.

When you have finished all the rows of peyote that you need, run the needle back down through the beads and out through the backing. Run the thread over toward the middle of the cab and knot off. By keeping the knots toward the middle you reduce the risk of accidentally trimming off a knot when you trim the backing or getting your needle stuck in a knot while beading the edge.

Trim the backing off at the edge of the beads forming the bezel.

Check the back side frequently to make sure you aren't cutting too close into your thread.

Your cabochon now has a completed bezel but still needs to be finished into some usable form. See the project chapter on page 33 for more on turning your cabochon into a finished pendant.

27

Even Count Peyote Bracelet

A diagonal pattern such as this is very easy to follow so it is a good first project. If you get mixed up and accidentally put a row too many or a row less in a color it is doubtful that anyone would ever notice.

Material & Supply List

Japanese cylinder beads size 10/0, four colors
Note: Bead quantities are given for one repeat, which equals approximately 2 inches. Multiply quantities by the number of repeats you will need to fit your wrist.

    #1 (shown in Dark Blue) 84 beads per repeat
    #2 (shown in Light Blue) 48 beads per repeat
    #3 (shown in Mauve) 48 beads per repeat
    #4 (shown in Fuchsia) 120 beads per repeat

Beading Thread and Needle
Scissors
Clasp of your choice

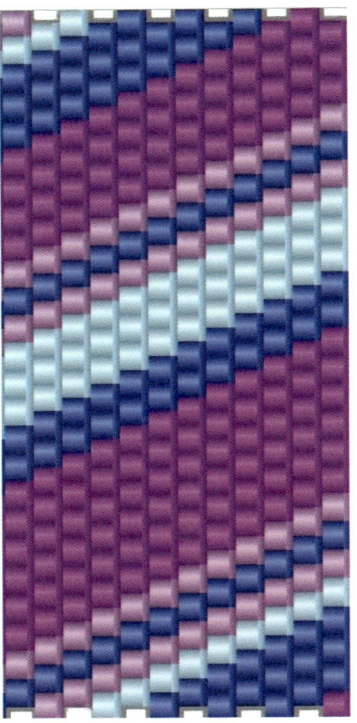

The pattern is shown as one repeat.

Start at the bottom left of the pattern.

String on one #1, two #3, two #2, six #1, and one #4 for row 1 & 2.

Follow the pattern until you reach the top of the repeat, then go back to the bottom of the pattern and work up again. Continue repeating the pattern until your bracelet is the desired length. Attach your clasp. The sample shown below used a magnetic bar clasp and a mix for color #4.

Odd Count Peyote Pendant

Material & Supply List

Japanese cylinder beads size 11/0 in 4 colors:
  #1 (shown Black) 449 beads
  #2 (shown Turquoise) 365 beads
  #3 (shown Coral) 329 beads
  #4 (shown Tan) 179 beads
Additional 1054 #1 for the bail
Coordinating beads for fringe
Beading Thread and Needle

This pattern is worked in odd count peyote stitch. Any time you have a centered design such as this one, the only way to get the center in the center is to use odd count!

Before you start working the pattern, work 34 rows of odd count peyote stitch with Color 1 for the bail. Leave about a foot of thread at the beginning of the bail section. Begin with 61 beads of Color 1 to make row 1 & 2, then work 32 more rows of odd count peyote. This will form the bail at the top of the pendant.

After you complete the beadwork for the bail section, begin the pattern, working the first row of the pattern into the last row of the bail section. You will be working the pendant from the top down: bail first and then pattern work with the diagonal section last. The pattern is shown upside down to make it easier to follow.

Lay a piece of paper or a ruler across the diagram to follow the pattern and check off the rows as you work so you don't lose your place. A geometric pattern is the easiest type to follow. Refer back to page 10 on decreasing at the end of rows, if needed to complete the angled section.

The Bail:
When you have finished the beadwork for the pendant, go back and put a needle on the foot of thread that you left at the beginning.

Curl the bail section over to the back and sew it down to the last row of #1 color before the pattern section. You will be "zipping" the beads together the same as you did in making tubular peyote beads.

This creates a tube at the top of the pendant to slide over a leather, chain, or other material to form the necklace. If you want to slide your pendant onto a heavier necklace, add more rows of #1 to make it as long as you want before you zip it down.

The Fringe:
When you finish the last row of the peyote pattern, add your fringe to the bottom. Attach your fringe to the cylinder beads extending from the bottom edge. This gives you eight drops in your fringe.

The sample shown here used 15/0 and 8/0 rocailles, 3mm bugle beads, and coral chips for the fringe.

Peyote Bead Bracelet

Material & Supply List:

Japanese cylinder beads size 11
  Main color 350 beads
  Accent color: 140 beads
  (shown in DB919 & DB610)
Japanese cylinder beads size 10
  About 50 in any color
6mm Glass Pearls: 10 beads
4mm Crystal bicones: 4 beads
6mm Metal Daisy Spacers: 10 beads
Beading Thread & Needle
Flexwire: about 1 foot
Clasp & Crimp Beads
Optional: wire protectors & crimp covers
Scissors, Crimp Tool

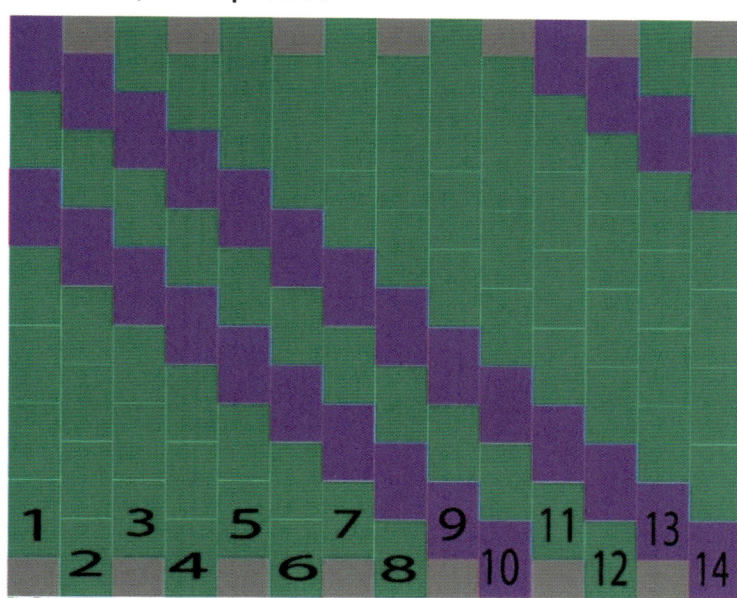

Start by making beads of flat tubular peyote stitch. Refer back to the basic instructions on page 16 if needed.

Following the pattern at left, make 5 beads. The row 1-2 sequence is numbered in order in the diagram.

Using the flex wire, string the beads into a bracelet:

Start with one pearl, then string on 1 daisy and the 1st peyote bead. Slide about 10 size 10 cylinder beads inside the peyote bead. This will help it keep its shape.

Make sure all the size 10 cylinder beads are completely inside the peyote tube so that when you put a daisy spacer on the 2nd end it will fit snuggly against the peyote bead.

String a daisy on each end of each peyote bead and a sequence of pearl, crystal, pearl between each peyote bead.

Finish off with one pearl at the other end.

Using the crimp beads, attach your clasp. Apply crimp covers if preferred.

The finished bracelet will have five peyote beads with a daily spacer on both ends and the pearls and crystals between.

As shown the bracelet measures 6 7/8 inches plus the clasp.

To adjust the length to longer or shorter:
　　Longer: use a larger clasp or add some extra silver spacers on each end of the crystals.
　　Shorter: use smaller pearls or crystals.
You can also adjust the length by making the peyote beads longer or shorter. This is easy to do if there is no pattern in the beads. If the beads have a pattern, as shown, then the pattern will have to be adapted for the longer or shorter length.

For a more dramatic size change add another peyote tube bead or take one out.

Cabochon Pendant with Beaded Bezel

Material and Supply List:

Cabochon
Japanese Cylinder Beads, Size 11
11/0 Rocailles
15/0 Rocailles
Glue-On Pendant Bail
Backing Material
Ultra-suede or Glove Leather
Beading Thread & Needle (Sharps recommended)
E6000 or similar Glue

(The cabochon shown is handmade fused glass, courtesy of the author's good friend Sharon.)

The quantity of beads needed will depend on the size of your cabochon.

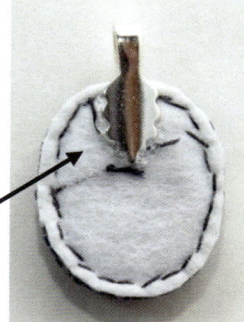

Bead your cabochon onto the backing. Refer back to Page 24 if needed.

Turn the beaded cab over and glue the pendant bail onto the back in the desired position.

Let the glue dry.

Apply glue to the back of the cabochon leaving about 1/16" - 1/8" space around the edge with no glue.

Press the glued cab firmly onto the WRONG side of your leather or ultra-suede. If using real leather make sure it is not too thick or it will be very difficult to bead through and leave a very think edge to cover. Glove leather works best.

Let the glue dry.

Carefully trim away the leather.

It should be even with the bead backing.

The bail will be sandwiched between the leather and the backing.

Tie a small sewing knot at the end of your thread.

Push the leather back from the edge and insert the needle through the bead backing only. This will leave the knot hidden between the two layers.

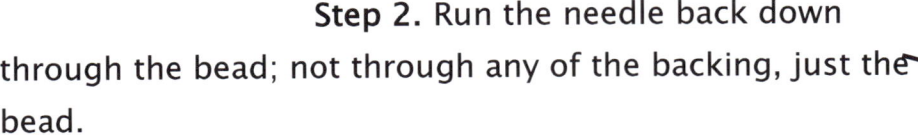

Step 1. String on one 11/0 rocaille.

Run the needle around the two layers and up through both layers. The thread will be exiting the bead backing in the same place as the first stitch.

Step 2. Run the needle back down through the bead; not through any of the backing, just the bead.

34

Step 3. With the thread coming out of the bottom of the bead, push the leather back again and run the needle up through the bead backing next to the first bead. The distance between this stitch and the last stitch through the backing should be about ¾ of the width of one bead.

You are now ready for the second bead.

Repeat steps 1-3 for the second bead.

Continue adding beads, each one repeating steps 1-3.

As you add beads you will see that the sandwich of layers pulls together, completely covering the bead backing layer inside.

The beads will sit at an angle.

Looking at the bezel from the front, the side edge of the beads will be visible. If you see the hole in the beads full on then you are spacing the beads too far apart.

The first bead will angle after you put on the last bead.

Continue beading until you are all the way around the cabochon. Knot off the thread into the edge of the sandwich. Run the needle into the sandwich and out at another point before you trim off the excess thread. It is always best not to trim the thread right next to a knot. If you have chosen your thread to match the backing, the stitches on the back will be barely visible.

The angled beads will completely cover the edge of the sandwich.

If the backing shows a bit around the bail, stitch a few 15/0 rocailles around the bail on the sides or front as needed.

Ruffled Peyote Bracelet

Material and Supply List:

Japanese Cylinder Beads, size 11
    About 1500 beads for 7"x 5/8"
11/0 Rocailles, about 450 for 7"
8/0 Rocailles, about 450 for 7"
Clasp of your Choice
    (5/8"Magnetic Bar shown)
Beading Thread & Needle
Scissors

This bracelet is worked end to end rather than back and forth. There are three ruffles: one down each side and one down the center. If you make your bracelet wider to accommodate a wider clasp, you might want to add a fourth ruffle down the middle.

Start by stringing enough Japanese cylinder beads to equal the desired length of your bracelet. When figuring length, don't forget to allow for the length of your clasp. Check to make sure that you have an EVEN number of beads (odd count peyote stitch would work just as well; it's just more work!).

Work at least 14 rows of peyote stitch into this base so that you have a total width of 16 rows or more. You can make the bracelet wider if needed to fit your clasp. If you make it narrower you may have trouble fitting in the center ruffle.

Depending on how your clasp attaches to the beadwork, it may be easier to add the clasp now before working the ruffles, as shown here.

Work the center ruffle first.

Stitch a row of cylinder beads down the center of the peyote base: Bring the thread

out of a cylinder bead at the end of the bracelet near the center of the base. String on one bead, skip over one bead in the base and run the needle through the next cylinder bead. Repeat down the length of the bracelet, stitching side to side in an undulating pattern as shown above.

When you look at the bracelet from the side there will be one bead size space between each of these beads.

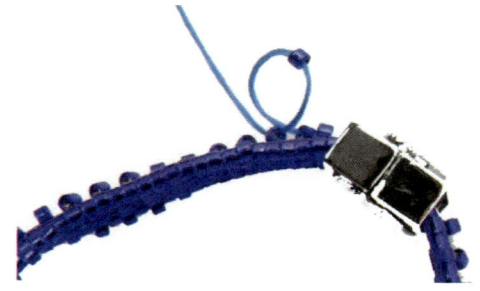

Work two rows of peyote stitch into this first row of beads.

Be sure and **work with the bracelet CURVED** into a bracelet shape. If you work with the bracelet flat the peyote rows can get too tight and the bracelet will be stiff. Keeping it curved allows the rows of cylinder beads to stand up in the center of the bracelet.

Continue the ruffle by working two rows of 11/0, followed by two rows of 8/0.

Be sure to pull each bead snuggly down between the two beads from the row before. This is what gives the ruffle its wave. If you work too loose the ruffle will be flat with thread showing.

When you have finished the center ruffle, work two rows of 11/0 and two rows of 8/0 down each side of the bracelet.

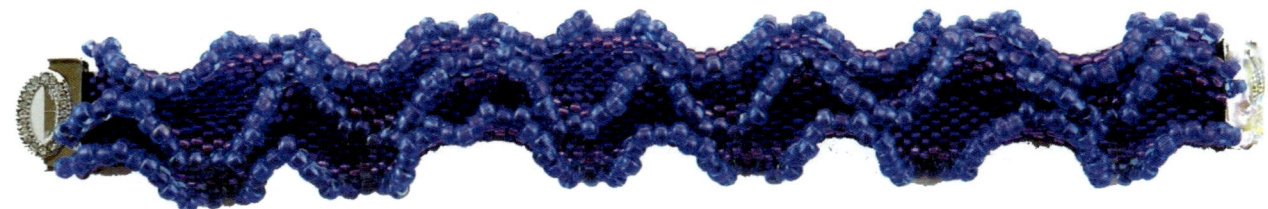

If desired you can embellish the bracelet by sewing crystals, pearls, or glass beads in among the ruffles.

For a different look, try grading the colors from one end to the other or from side to side or from the base to the tip of the ruffles.

For a wide bracelet, add more ruffles in the center.

Simple Spiral Bracelet

Material and Supply List:

11/0 Rocailles
  Color A: 240+ beads
  Color B: 160+ beads
  Color C: 80+ beads
Beading Needle and Thread
End caps
Clasp
Glue (a thick sticky one such as E-6000 or Zap Gel)

Leave about a foot of thread at the beginning.

String on 5 A, 2 B, 2 C, 2 B. Run the needle back through the 1st A, forming a circle.

Begin the peyote stitch with 3 A, B, C, B, working around the circle.

Repeat this pattern as many times as needed for the length of your bracelet (or necklace, if desired). There will be no beginning or end to rows, just keep going around in a circle.

Test your end caps to make sure they will fit on the spiral. If your caps are a bit too snug to fit over your spiral, work about three more rounds on each end, but decrease the size of the spiral by a couple of beads so that the tube is a bit smaller on each end. To finish, glue the end caps onto the ends of the peyote spiral and attach the clasp. **Let the glue dry.** Fasten the clasp onto the end caps.

This is a small enough tube that it will not need any filler for support. If you make a larger diameter spiral rope of peyote stitch it may need to be filled with a thick yarn or other material to keep from flattening.

Dimensional Spiral Necklace

Material and Supply List:

Japanese Cylinder Beads, about 600
11/0 Rocailles, about 280 beads
8/0 Rocailles, about 280 beads
8/0 Triangle Seed Beads, about 140 beads
Beads of your choice for front and back sections of the necklace (example shown used four strands of cylinder beads, 15/0, 11/0, and 8/0 rocailles with accents of 4mm and 8mm glass pearls, 8/0 triangles, and 10mm metal rondell beads for each end of the spirals)

Clasp
Flexwire, crimp beads, and crimp covers
Beading Thread and needles
Scissors, crimp tool

The peyote portion of this necklace begins with two spiral sections each about 3" long. One will be used on each side of the necklace. Note that to keep the necklace symmetrical the spiral turns to the left on one side and to the right on the other side.

The spiral will be worked the same as the Simple Spiral Bracelet, however this time instead of just changing the color you will be changing the bead size.

Each spiral starts out the same: Start by stringing on 19 cylinder beads; run the needle back through the 1st one to form a circle. Work two rows of peyote onto this 1st/2nd row base using only cylinder beads.

4th row: Instead of using 9 cylinder beads in this round, use 11/0, 8/0, triangle, 8/0, 11/0, and 4 cylinder beads.

Left Spiral: Work 68 rows of peyote, each time using the same bead as the bead the thread is coming OUT of. Finish up with 4 rows of just cylinder beads.

Right Spiral: Work 68 rows of peyote stitch, each time using the same bead as the bead the needle is going INTO. Finish up with four rows of just cylinder beads.

Tip: To keep track of your rows, first count out 68 triangle beads. When the triangles are used up you have finished your 68 rows.

Your spirals will have four rows of cylinder beads between the spirals of larger beads.

To finish your necklace:

Cut four pieces of wire at least 6" longer than you want the finished necklace. String your choice of beads onto the center section of each wire. In the example shown all four wires go through the metal bead at each end of the spirals. Run all four wire up through a spiral peyote section.

Continue beading the top section of the wires to get the finished length. Attach your clasp. The example shows all four wires passing through the last few beads on each side.

You can make an entire necklace of this dimensional spiral, however if you work with a tight tension needed to make the ridges pop, the necklace can get a bit stiff.

Diagonal Peyote Bracelet

This bracelet pattern uses a series of multiple-column increases and decreases to create a stepped bracelet. The pattern is shown in graded colors but could also be worked in a single color or alternating colors. The sample shown was worked with four colors.

Material and Supply List:

Japanese cylinder beads, size 11/0, 2 or more colors
    (Each square uses 100 beads, plus an additional 8 beads to finish the ends.)
Beading thread and needle
Scissors
Clasp of your choice
Embellishment beads (optional, not shown)

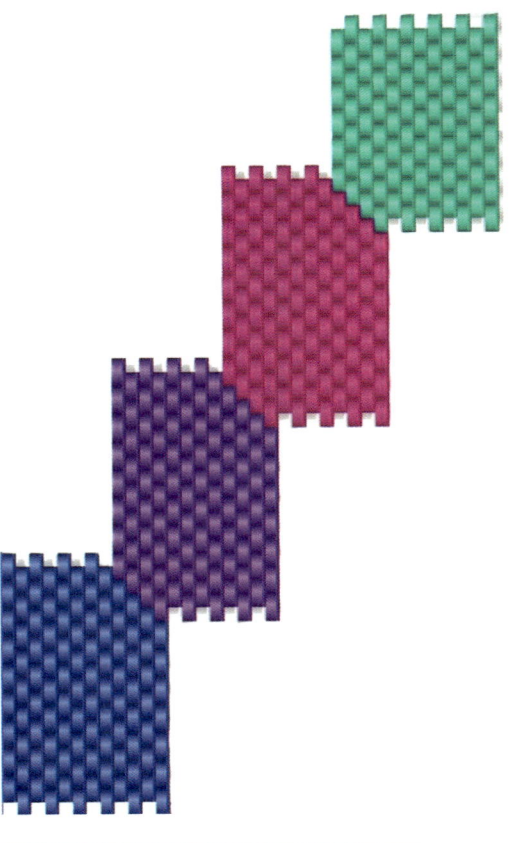

The diagram shows the first three squares and the fourth square to the point where the color change begins. The instructions will be given for color variation as shown, using four colors, designated as #1, #2, #3, #4. For a single color bracelet, work the pattern the same but ignore the color changes.

1. Start by stinging on 12 beads of #1 for rows 1-2. Work 12 more rows in #1.
2. Next row: 1 #2, 5 #1.
3. Next row: 5 #1, 1 #2, add 9 beads of #2 to make the increase of 8 columns (see pg. 11)

42

4. Work back across the increase and the top of the first square with 5 #2, 4 #1.
5. Next row: 4 #1, 6 #2.
6. 1st row of 2nd color only: work 6 #2.
7. Work 9 rows with #2.
8. Repeat steps 2–7, changing to colors #2 and #3, etc.

9. Continue until you have enough squares for the length you need for your bracelet.

Note: The sample shown with nine squares = 5.75 inches plus the clasp. Each additional square adds 5/8 inch to the length.

10. On the last square, finish the corner in the same color as the rest of the square by adding 4 more rows of the same color.

Tie off and bury any remaining thread ends.

Embellish edges if desired.

Attach clasp.

Russian Leaf Embellishment

Russian leaves are another variation of flat diagonal peyote stitch. It is important to keep the tension snug so that the leaves do not become too loose and floppy. Using one of the braided threads can help with this. Leaves can be made of varying sizes, with or without the larger beads on the edge for texture. Three variations are shown. This is NOT a beginner project! Practice simpler versions first. Refer back to page 14 if needed.

Material and Supply List:

Coordinating colors of rocailles, sizes 15/0, 11/0, and 8/0
Beading Thread and Needles
Scissors
Embellishment of your choice

Diagram guide:
  Green = 11/0 (#11)
  Brown = 8/0 (#8)
  Gold = 15/0 (#15)
  Gray = stopper bead

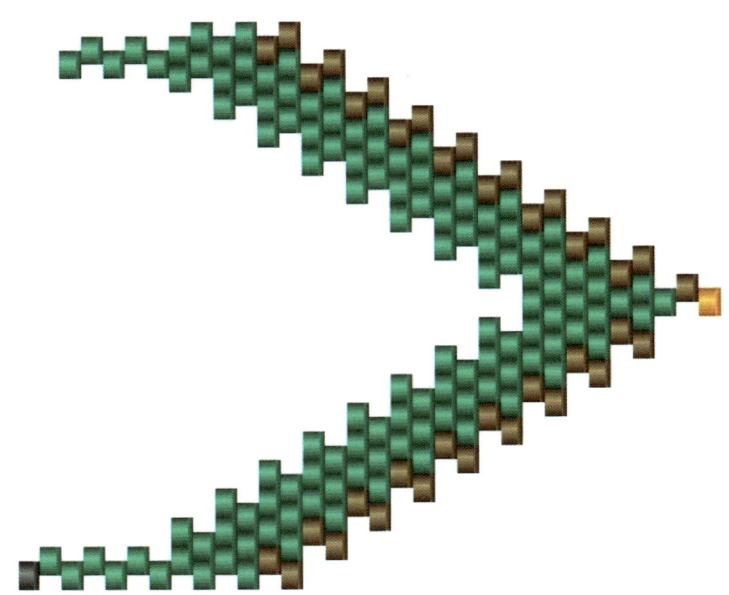

Large Leaf:

The large leaf (the background leaf in the finished sample shown above) will be made following the diagram.

Start at the lower left corner of the diagram with the stopper bead.

String on 10 #11 and 2 #8. This makes row 1 & 2.

Row 3, right to left: peyote stitches 3 #11

Row 4, left to right: 3 #11, then increase of #8, #8, #11.

Row 5, right to left: 2 #11

Repeat Row 4 and 5 until you have nine 9 pairs of 8/0 along the edge. Be sure to keep your tension snug!

Make one more row left to right but this time instead of the increase, string on #11, #8, #15. Go around the #15 and back through the #8 and #11.

This completes the bottom (left) half of the leaf. Now start the top (right) half. The increases will now be on the left side and the decreases will be on the right.

Row 21, right to left: 2 #11 plus increase with 3 #11.

Row 22, left to right: 1 #11, 1 #8.

Row 23: #8, 2 #11 plus increase with 3 #11.

Repeat row 22 and Row 23 until the top side of your leaf is the same length as the bottom side.

String on 5 #11. Run the needle through the 1st of the #11 on the other side (NOT the stopper bead). Tie the two thread ends together. Remove the stopper bead. This knot will not show in the finished project.

Your leaf should now look like this:

Medium Leaf:

This leaf will be made essentially the same as the large leaf, but with a different edging.

Row 1 & 2, left to right: Start with a stopper bead and string on 8 #11. Add an increase of #11 (#15, #8, #15), #11. The sequence in ( ) will be treated as one bead.

Row 3, right to left: 2 #11

Row 4, left to right: 3 #11 plus the increase of #11, (#15, #8, #15), #11.

Repeat Row 3 and 4 until you have 5 sets of #11, (#15, #8, #15) #11 down the side.

Work one more Row 4. At the end replace the increase sequence with #11, #15, #8, #15.

Skip the 2nd #15 and run the needle back through the 1st #11.

2nd half of leaf:

Row 1, second half of leaf, right to left: 2 #11 plus increase of 3 #11.

Row 2, second half, left to right: 2 #11, plus string on (#15, #8, #15) and treat as one bead.

Row 3, right to left: 2 #11, plus increase of 3 #11.

Repeat Row 2 & 3 until the 2nd side matches the 1st side.

At the end of the last row, string on three more #11 and run the needle back through the 1st #11 on the other side and tie the ends.

Veins in Large and Medium Leaves:

Leave the needle attached where you tied the two ends together. String on enough #15 to reach the bottom of the center of the leaf.

Take a stitch down and back up through the two beads at the bottom of the center opening.

Run the needle back up through a few of the #15.

String on enough #15 to reach one of the side beads on the leaf, loop through that bead and back up through these #15 beads.

Continue back up the leaf adding as many veins as you would like.

Small Leaf:

This smaller ruffled leaf is made the same as the other larger leaves with a couple of modifications:

Leave off the leading beads and start directly with the diagonal peyote section.

Leave off the embellishment beads on the edges: just make all the increases with 3 #11 beads.

Leave out the veins and sew the two inside edges of the leaf together. Zip it together like you did when making peyote tube beads. Pull the thread snug to make the leaf curl.

These small leaves can be made with any beads, however, they work especially well with 15/0 rocailles to make a more delicate leaf.

Leaves can be made individually and then fastened together to make an embellishment or they can be worked together, progressing from one bead to the next.

To finish the embellishment shown, sew all three leaves together, layering the smaller ones on top of the large one. Add other decorative beads as desired. The sample used a metal flower with a pearl in the center hole of the flower. This finished embellishment could be used as the center of a necklace, add a pin back to make a broach, or sew it onto your hat!

Zigzag Cuff Bracelet

This cuff is similar to working the pattern of diagonals in the flat even count peyote bracelet except you will be using varied sizes of beads. This will make the bracelet curve into a three dimensional cuff. The clasp will also be made of beads to match the bracelet.

Material and Supply List:

(About 5.5-7 repeats needed depending on size of wrist)

Japanese Cylinder Beads (shown in yellow): 144 per repeat
 +88 for end sections + 217 for clasp

11/0 Rocailles (shown in green): 72 per repeat +20 for end sections+ 13 for clasp

11/0 Triangle Beads (shown in blue): 72 per repeat

8/0 Rocailles (shown in red): 36 per repeat

Pattern will be worked from the bottom up.

Start here:

Row 1-2: string on 18 cylinder beads.
Row 3 & 4: work two rows of peyote with cylinder beads.
Row 5: 5 11/0 then 4 cylinder beads.
Row 6: 4 cylinder beads then 5 11/0.

You are now ready to start the repeats.
The first row at the bottom of the pattern at right will be the 7th row of your cuff.
When you finish the top row of this pattern then your next row will be the bottom row of the pattern again.

Work with your tension very snug and press the 8/0 rocailles (red) up from the bottom now and then to make sure that the raised portions of the cuff all stay on the same side of the bracelet.

Continue working the repeats as many times as necessary to make the cuff long enough for your wrist. You can't really measure the cuff in inches because of the curve, so just try it on now and then. To get the length correct you may need to use a half repeat at the end (finished sample shown has 5 ½ repeats).

At the end of the last repeat, leave off the last row of the pattern. Work the next row with 5 cylinder beads and then 4 11/0 rocailles. Work the next row with 4 11/0 rocailles then 5 cylinder beads. Finish with 4 rows of cylinder beads.

Loop End of clasp:

String on 26 cylinder beads for row 1-2. Work the 3rd row with cylinder beads and then work the 4th row with 11/0 rocailles. Pull your tension snug so that the 11/0 slip down between the cylinders, making the strip curve.

Sew the two ends of this curve to one end of the cuff.

Bar End of Clasp:

String on 20 cylinder beads for row 1-2.

Work rows 3 through 10 with cylinder beads and "Zip" up the cylinder. Tie off and bury the thread ends. This is the bar; set it aside until you finish the attachment shown next.

Attach a new thread to the end of the cuff without the curve, starting 6 beads from the edge. Stitch on three cylinder beads and then reverse. Keep adding three cylinder beads per row until you have a strip coming out from the end of the cuff that is 6 beads wide and 26 rows long.

Wrap this strip snuggly around the bar that you made and sew the end of the strip back down to itself to hold the bar in place. If your bar is loose, take a couple of stitches on each side to hold it in place.

Tie off and bury any remaining loose thread ends. Slip the bar through the curve to attach the bracelet.

~Not the End~

This is the end of this book but only the beginning of your adventures in creativity. There are endless possibilities with peyote stitch. Mix and match techniques and create wonderful things with your new skills. Keep on beading!

Printed in Great Britain
by Amazon